be

KIND

His Holiness the
Dalai Lama

HAMPTON ROADS

Hampton Roads Publishing Company, Inc.
Charlottesville, VA 22906

Distributed by Red Wheel/Weiser, LLC

www.redwheelweiser.com

Sign up for our newsletter and special offers by going to
www.redwheelweiser.com/newsletter.

ISBN: 978-1-64297-017-3

Library of Congress Control Number
available upon request

Printed in the United States of America
BP

10 9 8 7 6 5 4 3 2 1

With his characteristic down-to-earth approach to the Buddhist path, His Holiness the Dalai Lama has often observed of himself that his informal speaking style "complements my broken English." This volume has been edited to keep alive his voice and its unique flavor.

Publisher's note:

His Holiness the Dalai Lama describes himself as a simple monk. The hallmark of his tours and lectures worldwide is his warmth. With humor and simplicity, His Holiness speaks and answers questions on the enormous subject of our humanity—life, death, joy, illness, suffering, attachment, anger, compassion—but most of all, this simple monk tells us: Be kind.

The fundamental need we all have for kindness is evident in our repetition of one particular quote from the Dalai Lama; it is so often repeated on social media that the phrase has become a meme in its own right:

> "This is my simple religion. No need for temples. No need for complicated philosophy. Your own mind, your own heart is the temple. Your philosophy is simple kindness."

We all want to be treated with kindness. When we treat others with kindness, we feel fulfilled; we are, in that moment of grace, lifted out of whatever stressful day we've been dealing with. We feel good.

Kindness can be a smile, a friendly gesture, an act of generousity, a charitable donation, a moment of consideration for the needs of someone other than ourselves.

Whether we call it goodwill, affection, care, concern, or gentleness, the act of kindness has its roots in—and grows from—compassion.

His Holiness the Dalai Lama shares with us in this volume his teaching on compassion. He presents a path of giving and receiving and shows us a practical way of directing love and kindness.

In this little book, the Dalai Lama tells us, "Be kind."

Be kind whenever possible.

It is always possible.

KINDNESS

Compassion is the most wonderful and precious thing. When we talk about compassion, it is encouraging to note that basic human nature is, I believe, compassionate and gentle.

Sometimes I argue with friends who believe that human nature is more negative and aggressive. I argue that if you study the structure of the human body, you will see that it is akin to those species of mammals whose way of life is more gentle or peaceful.

Sometimes I half joke that our hands are arranged in such a manner that they are good for hugging, rather than hitting. If our hands were mainly meant for hitting, then these beautiful fingers would not be necessary. For example, if the fingers remain extended, boxers cannot hit forcefully, so they have to make fists.

So I think that means that our basic physical structure creates a compassionate or gentle kind of nature.

If we look at relationships, partnership, marriage, and conception are very important. Marriage should not be based on blind love or an extreme sort of mad love; it should be based on

"BASIC HUMAN NATURE

IS COMPASSIONATE

AND GENTLE."

a knowledge of one another and an understanding that you are suitable to live together.

Marriage is not for temporary satisfaction, but for some kind of sense of responsibility. That is the genuine love that is the basis of marriage.

The proper conception of a child takes place in that kind of moral or mental attitude. While the child is in the mother's womb, the mother's calmness of mind has a very positive effect on the unborn child, according to some scientists.

If the mother's mental state is negative—for instance if she is frustrated or angry—then it is very harmful to the healthy development of the unborn child.

One scientist has told me that the first few weeks after birth is the most important period, for during that time the child's brain is enlarging.

During that period, the mother's touch, or the touch of someone who is acting like a mother, is crucial.

This shows that even though the child may not realize who is who, it somehow physically needs someone else's affection. Without that, it is very damaging for the healthy development of the brain.

After birth, the first act by the mother is to give the child nourishing milk. If the mother lacks affection or kind feelings for the child, then the milk will not flow.

If the mother feeds her baby with gentle feelings toward the child, in spite of her own illness or pain, the milk flows freely.

This kind of attitude is like a precious jewel.

Moreover, from the other side, if the child lacks some kind of close feeling toward the mother, it may not suckle. This shows how wonderful the act of affection is from both sides.

"AFFECTION IS LIKE

A PRECIOUS JEWEL."

That is the beginning of our lives.

Similarly with education, it is my experience that those lessons that we learn from teachers who are not just good but who also show affection for the student, go deep into our minds. Lessons from other sorts of teachers may not. Although you may be compelled to study and may fear the teacher, the lessons may not sink in.

Much depends on the affection from the teacher.

Likewise, when we go to a hospital, irrespective of the doctor's quality, if the doctor shows genuine feeling and deep concern for us, and if he or she smiles, then we feel okay.

But if the doctor shows little human affection, then even though he or she may be a very great expert, we may feel unsure and nervous.

This is human nature.

Lastly, we can reflect on our lives. When we are young and again when we are old, we depend heavily on the affection of others.

Between these stages of childhood and old age, we usually feel that we can do everything without help from others and that affection from other people is simply not important.

But in these times, more than ever, I think it is very important to keep deep human affection—kindness is crucial to our society and to our survival.

When people in a big town or city feel lonely, this does not mean that they lack human companions, but rather that they lack human affection. As a result of this, their mental health eventually becomes very poor.

On the other hand, those people who grow up in an atmosphere of human

"KINDNESS IS CRUCIAL

TO OUR SOCIETY

AND TO OUR SURVIVAL."

affection have a much more positive and gentle development of their bodies, their minds, and their behavior.

Children who have grown up lacking that atmosphere usually have more negative attitudes.

This very clearly shows the basic human nature.

The human body appreciates peace of mind. Things that are disturbing to us have a very bad effect upon our health.

This shows that the whole structure of our health is such that it is suited to an atmosphere of human affection.

Therefore, our potential for compassion is there. The only issue is whether or not we realize this and utilize it.

The basic aim of my explanation is to show that by nature we are compassionate, that compassion is something very necessary, and it is something that we can develop.

What Is Compassion?

It is important to know the exact meaning of compassion. Different philosophies and traditions have different interpretations of the meanings of love and compassion.

Some of my Christian friends believe that love cannot develop without God's grace; in other words, to develop love and compassion you need faith.

The Buddhist interpretation is that genuine compassion is based on a clear acceptance or recognition that others, like oneself, want happiness and have the right to overcome suffering.

"GENUINE COMPASSION
IS BASED ON A RECOGNITION
THAT OTHERS, LIKE ONESELF,
WANT HAPPINESS."

"YOUR LOVE AND COMPASSION TOWARD YOUR FRIENDS IS, IN MANY CASES, ACTUALLY ATTACHMENT."

On that basis, one develops some kind of concern about the welfare of others, irrespective of one's attitude to oneself.

That is compassion.

However, your love and compassion toward your friends is, in many cases, actually attachment.

This feeling is not based on the realization that all beings have an equal right to be happy and to overcome suffering.

Instead, it is based on the idea that something is "mine," "my friend," or something good for "me."

That is attachment.

Thus, when that person's attitude toward you changes, your feeling of closeness immediately disappears.

Without attachment—that feeling of ownership—you develop some kind of concern irrespective of the other person's attitude to you, simply because that person is a fellow human being and has every right to overcome suffering.

Whether that person remains neutral to you or even becomes your enemy, your concern should remain because of his or her right.

That is the main difference.

Genuine compassion is much healthier; it is unbiased and it is based on reason. By contrast, attachment is narrow-minded and biased.

I will go so far as to say that attachment and genuine compassion are contradictory.

According to Buddhist practice, to develop genuine compassion you must first practice the meditation of equalization and equanimity, detaching youfself from those people who are very close to you.

"GENUINE COMPASSION IS

UNBIASED AND IT IS

BASED ON REASON . . . .

. . . BY CONTRAST,

ATTACHMENT IS

NARROW-MINDED AND BIASED."

Then, you must remove negative feelings toward your enemies. All sentient beings should be looked on as equal.

On that basis, you can gradually develop genuine compassion for all of them.

It must be said that genuine compassion is not like pity or a feeling that others are somehow lower than yourself. Rather, with genuine compassion, you view others as more important than yourself.

As I pointed out earlier, to generate genuine compassion, first of all one must go through the training of equanimity.

"WITH GENUINE COMPASSION

YOU VIEW OTHERS

AS MORE IMPORTANT

THAN YOURSELF."

This becomes very important, because without a sense of equanimity toward all, one's feelings toward others will be biased.

Equanimity

So now I will give you a brief example of a Buddhist meditative training on developing equanimity.

You should think about, first, a small group of people whom you know, such as your friends and relatives, toward whom you have attachment.

Second, you should think about some people to whom you feel totally indifferent.

And third, think about some people whom you dislike.

Once you have imagined these different people, you should try to let your mind go into its natural state and see how it would normally respond to an encounter with these people.

You will notice that your natural reaction would be that of attachment toward your friends, that of dislike toward the people whom you consider enemies and that of total indifference toward those whom you consider neutral.

Then you should try to question yourself. You should compare the effects of the two opposing attitudes you have toward your friends and your enemies,

"ALL SENTIENT BEINGS

SHOULD BE LOOKED

ON AS EQUAL."

and see why you should have such fluctuating states of mind toward these two different groups of people.

You should see what effects such reactions have on your mind and try to see the futility of relating to them in such an extreme manner.

I speak often of the pros and cons of harboring hatred and generating anger toward enemies, and I have also spoken a little about the defects of being extremely attached toward friends and so on.

You should reflect upon this and then try to minimize your strong emotions toward these two opposing groups of people.

Then, most importantly, you should reflect on the fundamental equality between yourself and all other sentient beings.

As you have the instinctive natural desire to be happy and overcome suffering, so do all sentient beings; just as you have the right to fullfil this innate aspiration, so do all sentient beings.

So on what exact grounds do you discriminate?

If we look at humanity as a whole, we are social animals. Moreover, the structures

"YOU SHOULD REFLECT ON
THE FUNDAMENTAL EQUALITY
BETWEEN YOURSELF AND ALL
OTHER SENTIENT BEINGS."

of the modern economy, education and so on, illustrate that the world has become a smaller place and that we heavily depend on one another.

Under such circumstances, I think the only option is to live and work together harmoniously and keep in our minds the interest of the whole of humanity.

That is the only outlook and path we must adopt for our survival.

By nature, especially as a human being, my interests are not independent of others. My happiness depends on others' happiness.

So when I see happy people, automatically I also feel a little bit happier than when I see people in a difficult situation.

For example, when we see pictures on television that show people starving in Somalia, including old people and young children, then we automatically feel sad, regardless of whether that sadness can lead to some kind of active help or not.

Moreover, in our daily lives, we are now utilizing many good facilities, including things like air-conditioned houses. All these things or facilities became possible, not because of ourselves, but

"MY INTERESTS ARE NOT
INDEPENDENT OF OTHERS.
MY HAPPINESS DEPENDS
ON OTHERS' HAPPINESS."

"THE ONLY OPTION

IS TO LIVE AND

WORK TOGETHER

HARMONIOUSLY."

because of many other people's direct or indirect involvement.

Everything comes together. It is impossible to return to the way of life of a few centuries ago, when we depended on simple instruments and not all these machines.

It is very clear to us that the facilities that we are enjoying now are the products of the activities of many people.

Most of you sleep on a bed—many people have been involved in the making of that. Also in the preparation of your food, especially for the non-vegetarian.

Fame is definitely a product of other people—without the presence of other people, the concept of fame would not even make sense.

Also, the interest of Europe depends on America's interest, and Western Europe's interest depends on the Eastern European economic situation.

Each continent is heavily dependent on the others—that is the reality. Thus many of the things that we desire, such as wealth, fame, and so forth, could not come into being without the active or indirect participation and cooperation of many other people.

"COMPASSION IS NOT A QUESTION

OF RELIGIOUS PRACTICE,

BUT A QUESTION OF THE FUTURE

OF HUMANITY."

Therefore, since we all have an equal right to be happy and since we are all linked to one another, no matter how important an individual is, logically the interest of the other nearly eight billion people on the planet is more important than that of one single person.

By thinking along these lines, you can eventually develop a sense of global responsibility.

Modern environmental problems, such as the depletion of the ozone layer and global warming, also clearly show us the need for world co-operation.

It seems that with development, the whole world has become much smaller, but the human consciousness is still lagging behind.

This is not a question of religious practice, but a question of the future of humanity.

"ALTRUISM KEEPS US
FROM BEING INDIFFERENT
TO OTHERS."

Altruism

This kind of wider or more altruistic attitude is very relevant in today's world.

If we look at the situation from various angles, such as the complexity and interconnectedness of the nature of modern existence, then we will gradually notice a change in our outlook, so that when we say "others" and when we think of others, we will no longer dismiss them as something that is irrelevant to us. We will no longer feel indifferent.

If you think only of yourself, if you forget the rights and well-being of others, or, worse still, if you exploit others, ultimately you will lose.

You will have no friends who will show concern for your well-being. Moreover, if a tragedy befalls you, instead of feeling concerned, others might even secretly rejoice.

By contrast, if an individual is compassionate and altruistic, and has the interests of others in mind, then irrespective of whether that person knows a lot of people, wherever that person moves, he or she will immediately make friends.

"TRUE FRIENDSHIP

DEVELOPS ON THE BASIS

OF GENUINE HUMAN

AFFECTION."

And when that person faces a tragedy, there will be plenty of people who will come to help.

A true friendship develops on the basis of genuine human affection, not money or power.

Of course, due to your power or wealth, more people may approach you with big smiles or gifts. But deep down, these are not real friends of yours—these are friends of your wealth or power.

As long as your fortune remains, then these people will often approach you. But when your fortunes decline, they will no longer be there.

With this type of friend, nobody will make a sincere effort to help you if you need it. That is the reality.

Genuine human friendship is on the basis of human affection, irrespective of your position.

Therefore, the more you show concern about the welfare and rights of others, the more you are a genuine friend.

The more you remain open and sincere, then ultimately more benefits will come to you.

If you forget or do not bother about others, then eventually you will lose your own benefit.

So sometimes I tell people, if we really are selfish, then wise selfishness is much better than the selfishness of ignorance and narrow-mindedness.

Wisdom

For Buddhist practitioners, the development of wisdom is very important—and here I mean wisdom that realizes *Shunya,* the ultimate nature of reality.

The basic fact is that all sentient beings, particularly human beings, want happiness and do not want pain and suffering.

As humans, we all have the same human potential.

The wonderful human brain is the source of our strength and the source of our future, provided we utilize it in the right direction.

"ALL SENTIENT BEINGS WANT HAPPINESS."

The human brain allows us to create happy lives for ourselves and also to help other beings.

It is my belief that the human brain and basic human compassion are by nature in some kind of balance.

Sometimes, when we grow up, we may neglect human affection and simply concentrate on the human brain, thus losing the balance. It is then that disasters and unwelcome things happen.

With the realization of one's own potential and self-confidence in one's ability, one can build a better world.

"THE HUMAN BRAIN AND
BASIC HUMAN COMPASSION
ARE BY NATURE IN SOME
KIND OF BALANCE."

According to my own experience, self-confidence is very important.

That sort of confidence is not a blind one: it is an awareness of one's own potential. On that basis, human beings can transform themselves by increasing the good qualities and reducing the negative qualities.

Transformation does not mean 100 percent change. Without a basis of something to aim for, how do we develop good things?

Buddhists call this potential "Buddha Nature," which is also the fundamental Clear Light nature of the mind.

"THE HUMAN BRAIN

ALLOWS US TO CREATE

HAPPY LIVES FOR OURSELVES

AND ALSO TO HELP

OTHER BEINGS."

The fundamental teaching of the Buddha is on the Four Noble Truths: 1) there is suffering; 2) suffering has cause; 3) there is cessation of suffering; and, finally, 4) there is a path to this freedom from suffering.

The underlying principle of this teaching is the universal principle of causality.

What becomes important in the understanding of this basic teaching is a genuine awareness of one's own potentials and the need to utilize them to their fullest.

Seen in this light, every human action becomes significant.

For example, the smile is a very important feature of the human face. But because of human intelligence, even that good part of human nature can be used in the wrong way, such as sarcastic smiles, or diplomatic smiles, which only serve to create suspicion.

I feel that a genuine, affectionate smile is very important in our day-to-day lives.

How one creates that smile largely depends on one's own attitude. It is illogical to expect smiles from others if one does not smile oneself.

Therefore, one can see that many things depend on one's own behavior.

"A GENUINE, AFFECTIONATE
SMILE IS VERY IMPORTANT IN
OUR DAY-TO-DAY LIVES."

The realization of *Shunya* gives you at least some kind of positive sense about cessation.

Once you have some kind of feeling for the possibility of cessation, then it becomes clear that suffering is not final and that there is an alternative.

If there is alternative, then it is worth making an effort.

If only two of the Buddha's Four Noble Truths exist, suffering and the cause of suffering, then there is not much meaning. But the other two Noble Truths, including cessation, point toward an alternative way of existence.

There is possibility of ending suffering. So it is worthwhile to realize the nature of suffering.

Therefore wisdom is extremely important in increasing compassion infinitely.

So that is how one engages in the practice of Buddhism: there is an application of the faculty of wisdom, using intelligence, and an understanding of the nature of reality, together with the skilful means of generating compassion.

"SUFFERING IS NOT FINAL

AND THERE IS

AN ALTERNATIVE. . . .

. . . IF THERE IS

AN ALTERNATIVE, THEN

IT IS WORTH MAKING

AN EFFORT."

Kindness in the Real World

I think that in your daily lives and in all sorts of your professional work, you can use this compassionate motivation.

Of course, in the field of education, there is no doubt that compassionate motivation is important and relevant.

Irrespective of whether you are a believer or nonbeliever, compassion for the students' lives or futures—not just a focus on the outcome of their examinations—makes your work as a teacher much more effective.

"EVERY HUMAN ACTION

BECOMES SIGNIFICANT."

With that motivation through kindness and compassion, I think your students will remember you for the whole of their lives.

Similarly, in the field of health, there is an expression in Tibetan that says that the effectiveness of the treatment depends on how warm-hearted the physician is.

Because of this expression, when treatments from a certain doctor do not work, people blame the doctor's character, speculating that perhaps that he or she was not a kind person.

"ALL SOCIAL SYSTEMS

BENEFIT FROM KINDNESS

AND COMPASSION."

The poor doctor sometimes gets a very bad name! So in the medical field, there is no doubt that compassionate motivation is something very relevant.

I think this is also the case with lawyers and politicians. If politicians and lawyers had more compassionate motivation, then there would be less scandal. And, as a result, the whole community would get more peace.

I think the work of politics would become more effective and more respected.

Finally, in my view, the worst thing is warfare.

Warfare has become very detached from human to human contact—there are drones, airstrikes, and mechanisms of all kinds.

However horrible, even warfare with human affection and with human compassion is much less destructive.

Completely mechanized warfare that is without human feeling is worse.

Also, I think compassion and a sense of responsibility can also enter into the fields of science and engineering.

Of course, from a purely scientific point of view, awful weapons such as nuclear bombs are remarkable achievements.

But we can say that these are negative because they bring immense suffering to the world.

Therefore, if we do not take into account human pain, human feelings, and human compassion, there is no demarcation between right and wrong.

Therefore, human compassion can reach everywhere.

I find it a little bit difficult to apply this principle of compassion to the field of economics. But economists are human beings and of course they also need human affection, without which they would suffer.

"HUMAN COMPASSION

CAN REACH EVERYWHERE."

However, if you think only of profit, irrespective of the consequences, then drug dealers are not wrong, because, from the economic viewpoint, they are also making tremendous profits.

But because this is very harmful for society and for the community, we call this wrong and name these people criminals.

If that is the case, then I think arms dealers are in the same category. The arms trade is equally dangerous and irresponsible.

So I think for these reasons, human compassion, or what I sometimes call

"HUMAN AFFECTION IS

THE KEY FACTOR FOR ALL

HUMAN BUSINESS."

"human affection," is the key factor for all human business.

Just as you see that with the palm of our hand all five fingers become useful, if these fingers were not connected to the palm they would be useless.

Similarly, every human action that is without human feeling becomes dangerous.

With human feeling and an appreciation of human values, all human activities become constructive.

Even religion, which is supposedly good for humanity, without that basic

"EVERY HUMAN ACTION

THAT IS WITHOUT

HUMAN FEELING

BECOMES DANGEROUS."

human compassionate attitude can become foul.

Unfortunately, even now, there are problems that are entirely down to different religions.

So human compassion is something fundamental. If that is there, then all other human activities become more useful.

Motivating Kindness

Generally speaking, I have the impression that in education and some other areas there is some negligence of the issue of human motivation.

Perhaps in ancient times religion was supposed to carry this responsibility. But now in the community, religion generally seems a little bit old-fashioned, so people are losing interest in it and in deeper human values.

However, I think these should be two separate things.

If you have respect for or interest in religion, that is good. But even if you have no interest in religion, you should not forget the importance of these deeper human values.

There are various positive side-effects of enhancing one's feeling of compassion.

One of them is that the greater the force of your compassion, the greater your resilience in confronting hardships and your ability to transform them into more positive conditions.

One form of practice that seems to be quite effective is found in *A Guide to* the Bodhisattva Way of Life, a classic Buddhist text.

In this practice, you visualize your old self—the embodiment of self-centredness, selfishness, and so on—and then visualize a group of people who represent the masses of other sentient beings.

Then you adopt a third person's point of view as a neutral, unbiased observer and make a comparative assessment of the value, the interests, and then the importance of these two groups.

Also try to reflect upon the faults of being totally oblivious to the well-being

"THE GREATER THE FORCE OF YOUR COMPASSION, THE GREATER YOUR RESILIENCE IN CONFRONTING HARDSHIPS . . .

. . . AND THE GREATER YOUR ABILITY

TO TRANSFORM THEM

INTO MORE POSITIVE CONDITIONS."

of other sentient beings and so on, and what this old self has really achieved as a result of leading such a way of life.

Then reflect on the other sentient beings and see how important their well-being is, the need to serve them and so forth, and see what you, as a third neutral observer, would conclude as to whose interests and well-being are more important.

You would naturally begin to feel more inclined toward the countless others.

I also think that the greater the force of your altruistic attitude toward sentient beings, the more courageous you become.

The greater your courage, the less you feel prone to discouragement and loss of hope.

Therefore, compassion is also a source of inner strength.

With increased inner strength, it is possible to develop firm determination, and with determination, there is a greater chance of success, no matter what obstacles there may be.

On the other hand, if you feel hesitation, fear, and a lack of self-confidence, then

"THE GREATER YOUR

ALTRUISTIC ATTITUDE

TOWARD SENTIENT BEINGS,

THE MORE COURAGEOUS

YOU BECOME. . . .

. . . THE GREATER YOUR COURAGE,

THE LESS YOU FEEL

DISCOURAGED AND HOPELESS."

often you will develop a pessimistic attitude.

I consider that to be the real seed of
failure.

With a pessimistic attitude, you cannot
accomplish even something you should
be able to easily achieve.

Whereas even if something is difficult
to achieve, if you have an unshakeable
determination, there is eventually the
possibility of achievement.

Therefore, even in the conventional
sense, compassion is very important for
a successful future.

As I pointed out earlier, depending on the level of your wisdom, there are different levels of compassion, such as compassion that is motivated by genuine insight into the ultimate nature of reality, compassion that is motivated by the appreciation of the impermanent nature of existence, and compassion that is motivated by awareness of the suffering of other sentient beings.

The level of your wisdom, or the depth of your insight into the nature of reality, determines the level of compassion that you will experience.

From the Buddhist viewpoint, compassion with wisdom is essential. It is as if

"FROM THE BUDDHIST VIEWPOINT, COMPASSION WITH WISDOM IS ESSENTIAL."

compassion is like a very honest person and wisdom is like a very able person; if you join these two, then the result is something very effective.

Finding Common Ground

I see compassion, love, and forgiveness as common ground for all different religions, irrespective of tradition or philosophy.

Although there are fundamental differences between different religious ideas, such as the acceptance of an Almighty Creator, every religion teaches us the same message: be a warm-hearted person.

All of them emphasize the importance of compassion and forgiveness.

"COMPASSION, LOVE, AND FORGIVENESS CREATE COMMON GROUND FOR ALL DIFFERENT RELIGIONS."

Now, in ancient times, when the various religions were based in different places and there was less communication between them, there was no need for pluralism among the various religious traditions.

But today, the world has become much smaller, so communication between different religious faiths has become very strong. Under such circumstances, I think pluralism among religious believers is essential.

Through unbiased, objective study, you can see the value these different religions have had to humanity through the centuries. Once you see this value, then there is plenty of reason to accept or to respect all these different religions.

After all, in humanity there are many different mental dispositions, so simply one religion, no matter how profound, cannot satisfy all the variety of people.

For instance, now, in spite of such a diversity of religious traditions, the majority of people still remain unattracted by religion.

Of the nearly eight billion people, I believe only around one billion are true religious believers.

The majority of people may identify with a religion, and they may say, "My family background is Christian, Muslim, or Buddhist; therefore I'm a Christian, Muslim, or Buddhist."

But for these people, when they say, for example, "I am Christian," then only during that moment of saying it aloud do they remember God, pray to God, and are concious to not let out negative emotions.

However, true believers practice their religion in their daily lives, and particularly when some difficult situation arises.

They do not have to say they are followers of a particular religion. They do not have to think it. They live their religion in their actions.

Of these true believers, I think there are perhaps less than one billion. The rest of humanity, more than six billion people, remain, in the true sense, non-believers.

So one religion obviously cannot satisfy all of humanity.

Under such circumstances, a variety of religions is actually necessary and useful, and therefore the only sensible thing is that all different religions work together and live harmoniously, helping one another.

There have been positive develop-
ments recently, and I have noticed
closer relations forming between various religions.

Giving and Taking

So, having reflected upon the faults of a self-centered life and way of thinking, and also having reflected upon the positive consequences of being mindful of the well-being of other sentient beings and working for their benefit, and being convinced of this, then in Buddhist meditation there is a special training that is known as "the practice of Giving and Taking."

This is especially designed to enhance your power of compassion and love toward other sentient beings.

It basically involves visualizing taking upon yourself all the suffering, pain, negativity, and undesirable experiences of other sentient beings.

Imagine taking these upon yourself and then giving away or sharing with others your own positive qualities, such as your virtuous states of mind, your positive energy, your wealth, your happiness, and so forth.

Such a form of training cannot actually result in a reduction of suffering by other sentient beings or a production of your own positive qualities. But this training psychologically brings about a transformation in your mind so effectively that your feeling of love and compassion is much more enhanced.

Trying to implement this practice in your daily life is quite powerful and can be a very positive influence on your mind and on your health.

If you feel that it seems worthwhile to practice, then irrespective of whether you are a believer or a nonbeliever, you should try to promote these basic human good qualities.

One thing you should remember is that these mental transformations take time and are not easy.

I think some people from Western cultures, where technology is so good, think that everything is automatic.

Kindness is not automatic.

You should not expect this spiritual transformation to take place within a short period; that is impossible.

Keep it in your mind and make a constant effort. Then after one year, five years, ten years, fifteen years, you will eventually find some change.

I still sometimes find it very difficult to practice these things. However, I really do believe that these practices are extremely useful.

My favorite quotation from Shantideva's book is:

> "So long as sentient beings remain, so long as space remains, I will remain in order to serve, or in order to make some small contribution for the benefit of others."

Titles in This Series

Be Happy

Be Angry

Be Here

Be Kind

About the Author

His Holiness the fourteenth Dalai Lama, Tenzin Gyatso, is the spiritual and temporal leader of the Tibetan people. He has written a number of books on Buddhism and philosophy and has received many international awards, including the 1989 Nobel Peace Prize.